DEC 0 7 2012

W9-DAL-790

Easy Quilts *for* Beginners *and* Beyond

Easy Quilts *for* Beginners *and* Beyond

14
Quilt Patterns
from
Quiltmaker
MAGAZINE

Martingale®
Create with Confidence

Easy Quilts for Beginners and Beyond:
14 Quilt Patterns from *Quiltmaker* Magazine
© 2012 by *Quiltmaker*

Martingale®
19021 120th Ave. NE, Ste. 102
Bothell, WA 98011-9511 USA
ShopMartingale.com

Mission Statement

Dedicated to providing quality products and service to inspire creativity.

Quiltmaker, ISSN 1047-1634, is published bimonthly by Creative Crafts Group, LLC, 741 Corporate Circle, Suite A, Golden, CO 80401, www.quiltmaker.com.

Printed in China
17 16 15 14 13 12   8 7 6 5 4 3 2 1

Library of Congress Cataloging-in-Publication Data is available upon request.

ISBN: 978-1-60468-237-3

Credits

President & CEO: Tom Wierzbicki
Editor in Chief: Mary V. Green
Design Director: Paula Schlosser
Managing Editor: Karen Costello Soltys
Technical Editor: Ellen Pahl
Copy Editor: Marcy Heffernan
Production Manager: Regina Girard
Illustrator: Ann Marra
Cover Designer: Paula Schlosser
Text Designer: Connor Chin
Layout Artist: Dianna Logan / DBS
Photographer: Mellissa Karlin Mahoney,
     except page 39 by Joe Hancock Studio

Contents

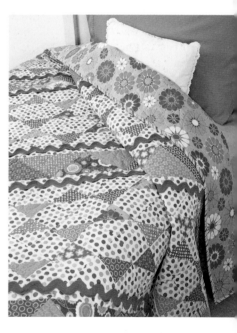

Introduction

Whether you're a beginning quiltmaker, or one who's been around the quilt block once or twice, you'll find many delightful patterns in this book. The best part is that easy doesn't mean boring. These quilts all have interesting designs, but were carefully selected for their ease in construction.

What makes a quilt easy to make?

- large patches of beautiful fabric

- simple designs with few seams to match

- quick techniques like chain piecing and half-square triangles

- freeform piecing

When I first started quilting, I only selected patterns with squares and rectangles. Then I tried a quilt that had triangles made from half-square triangles and I realized they're not hard at all. I was still sewing squares together with a straight seam, but my quiltmaking possibilities had suddenly expanded!

The next significant lesson on my quiltmaking journey? Fusible appliqué. I started with simple shapes and gentle curves, and pretty soon realized I could also appliqué.

What's next for you? Give any of these patterns with our complete step-by-step instructions a try. I'm sure you'll soon be adding more techniques to your quiltmaking adventures.

Enjoy!
June Dudley
Editor-in-Chief
Quiltmaker

These dazzling asterisk blocks look complicated, but they're really quite easy to make. And the scrappy striped border contains them all nicely. This is a perfect design for the quilter with a big scrap collection!

Materials

Yardage is based on 42"-wide fabric.

6⅞ yards *total* of assorted prints for blocks and pieced middle border

⅞ yard *total* of assorted black prints for pieced middle border

⅝ yard of red tone-on-tone print for inner and outer borders

⅝ yard of black-and-red print for binding

4⅓ yards of fabric for backing

72" x 72" piece of batting

Cutting

From the assorted prints, cut:
81 squares, 7" x 7"
81 strips, 1" x 42"
234 rectangles, 1" x 4"

From the red tone-on-tone print, cut:
6 strips, 1" x 42"
7 strips, 1½" x 42"

From the assorted black prints, cut:
234 rectangles, 1" x 4"

From the black-and-red print, cut:
7 strips, 2¼" x 42"

Finished throw: *64" x 64"* | **Finished blocks:** *6" x 6"*

Making the Blocks

These blocks may look complex, but they're quick and easy to make. Press all of the seam allowances toward the narrow strips.

1. Choose one 7" square and a contrasting 1" x 42" strip. Cut the strip crosswise into four approximately equal lengths. Use a ruler and rotary cutter to slice diagonally across the square. Sew the contrasting strip between the two triangles as shown. Your strip

will extend beyond the ends of the square; they'll be trimmed later. Press the seam allowances toward the strip.

2. Cut the unit from step 1 in half diagonally in the opposite direction as shown; sew another strip between the halves and press.

3. Cut the unit in half vertically and add a third strip in the same way. Press.

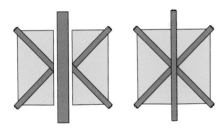

4. Cut the unit in half horizontally and add the final strip as shown. Press.

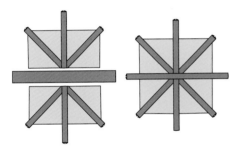

5. Trim the block to 6½" x 6½". A 6½" square ruler makes this task really easy! Align the 3¼" marks on the ruler with the block center as shown and trim all the sides, rotating the block for cutting as needed.

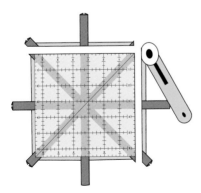

6. Repeat steps 1–5 to make a total of 81 blocks.

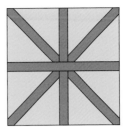

Make 81.

Assembling the Quilt Top

1. Use a design wall to arrange the blocks in nine rows of nine blocks each. Join the blocks into rows as shown in the quilt assembly diagram on page 10. Press the seam allowances in opposite directions from row to row. Sew the rows together and press. The quilt top should measure 54½" x 54½".

Color Option

Making these little babies was a lot like eating candy—hard to stop! Use many values and a variety of scales for a successful scrappy look. Set five by six, this sweet little quilt is perfect for an even sweeter baby.

2. Join the 1"-wide red strips end to end and cut two lengths of 54½"; sew them to the sides of the quilt. Press the seam allowances toward the red strips. Cut two lengths of 55½"; join them to the top and bottom of the quilt and press.

3. For each pieced side border, join 110 rectangles, alternating black-print and colored rectangles as shown. For the top and bottom borders, join 124 rectangles, again alternating black-print and colored rectangles. Press all seam allowances in the same direction.

4. Matching centers and ends, sew the pieced border strips to the sides of the quilt. Then join the top and bottom pieced borders to the top and bottom of the quilt. Press the seam allowances toward the red border.

5. Join the 1½"-wide red strips end to end and cut two lengths of 65" for the sides and two lengths of 67" for the top and bottom. Sew the side border strips to the quilt and trim any extra length. Press the seam allowances toward the red border. Add the top and bottom border strips, trim, and press.

Quilting and Finishing

For more information on quilting and finishing your quilt, refer to "Basic Quiltmaking Lessons" on page 74.

1. Layer and baste together the backing, batting, and quilt top.

2. Quilt waving lines across the entire quilt surface as shown in the quilting placement diagram.

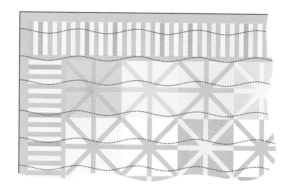

Quilting placement

3. Bind the quilt using the 2¼"-wide black-and-red strips.

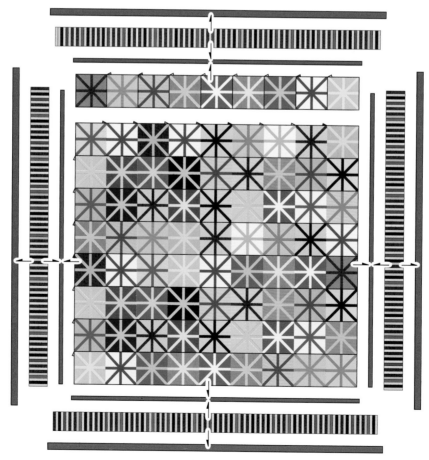

Quilt assembly

Snuggle your beach baby in this cozy wrap. Backed with terry cloth, it's tailor-made for the shore or the pool. Of course, it could just as easily be made into a quick and colorful crib quilt for that special baby or toddler. (See the color option, opposite.)

Materials

Yardage is based on 42"-wide fabric unless otherwise noted.

- 1¼ yards *total* of assorted bright prints for strips and binding
- 1 yard of white tone-on-tone print for sashing and borders
- 1½ yards of white terry cloth (45" wide) for backing

Cutting

From the assorted bright prints, cut:
15 strips, 2½" x 42"

From the white tone-on-tone print, cut:
9 strips, 2½" x 42"
2 strips, 4" x 37"

From the white terry cloth, cut:
1 rectangle, 38" x 47"

Finished quilt: 34" x 43"

Assembling the Quilt Top

1. Cut each of the 15 assorted bright-print strips into three pieces ranging from 11" to 17" long. Join the pieces with diagonal seams as shown to make one long strip. Sew all of the diagonal seams in the same direction. Trim the seam allowances to ¼" and press them all in the same direction.

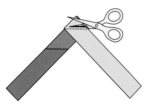

2. From the pieced strip, cut eight lengths of about 40" each. Set aside the remainder of the long strip to use for the binding.

3. Arrange the pieced strips and the nine 2½" x 42" sashing strips vertically into a pleasing composition. Begin and end with a white sashing strip. Join the sashing and the pieced strips, and press the seam allowances toward the darker strips. Trim the quilt to 36½" from top to bottom.

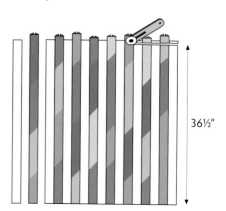

36½"

4. Add the 4" x 37" border strips to the top and bottom, trimming any extra length.

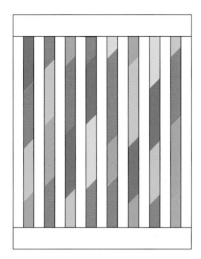

Quilt assembly

Quilting and Finishing

For more information on quilting and finishing your quilt, refer to "Basic Quiltmaking Lessons" on page 74.

1. Layer the quilt top with the terry-cloth backing wrong sides together and baste. (This quilt does not have batting.)

2. Quilt the pieced strips and sashing in the ditch. Use the leftover pieced strip to bind the quilt. Off to the beach!

Quilting placement

Color Option

This pattern also works well with batting and a regular fabric backing in place of the terry cloth. Lots of bright, fun fabrics combine with a polka-dot print to make a happy baby quilt.

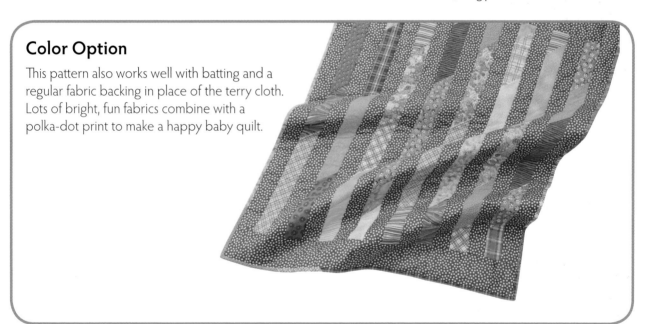

Coin Collecting

Designed by Rachel Griffin; sewn by Carolyn St. Clair; quilted by Maggi Honeyman

Make a fun quilt with stacks of change. Think of this as "coins gone wild." The blocks are free to just be wild, but in a structured way. Choose a collection of favorite fabrics or dig into your stash for leftover strips to make a scrappy version using your spare change.

Materials

Yardage is based on 42"-wide fabric.

2⅜ yards of cream print for blocks and border

2⅛ yards *total* of assorted blue, brown, and cream prints*

⅝ yard of blue print for binding

3⅞ yards of fabric for backing

63" x 78" piece of batting

Or 45 strips, 1½" x 42"

Cutting

From the assorted blue, brown, and cream prints, cut:
90 strips, 1½" x 21"

From the cream print, cut *on the lengthwise grain:*
2 strips, 5½" x 63"
2 strips, 5½" x 58"

From the remainder of the cream print, cut:
12 rectangles, 3½" x 15½"
24 rectangles, 2" x 15½"

From the blue print, cut:
7 strips, 2¼" x 42"

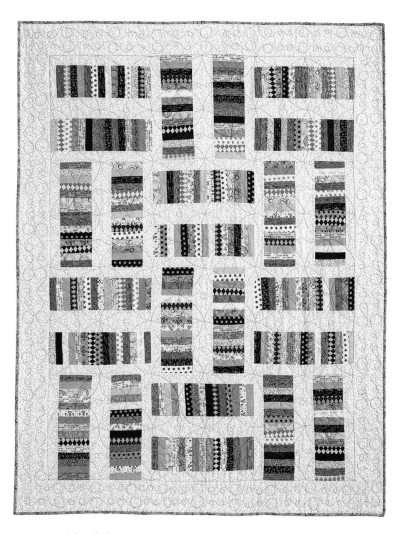

Finished throw: 55" x 70" | **Finished blocks:** 15" x 15"

Making the Blocks

1. Sew 15 assorted strips together randomly to make a strip set as shown. Press the seam allowances in one direction. Make six strip sets. Cut the strip sets at 5" intervals to make 24 units.

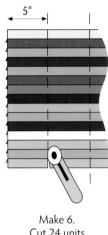

Make 6.
Cut 24 units.

2. Sew two units from step 1, two cream 2" x 15½" rectangles, and one cream 3½" x 15½" rectangle together as shown to make a block. Press the seam allowances toward the cream rectangles. Make 12 blocks.

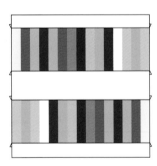

Make 12.

Assembling the Quilt

1. Arrange the blocks into four rows of three blocks each, alternating the orientation of the blocks as shown. Sew the blocks into rows. Press the seam allowances toward the vertical blocks. Sew the rows together and then press seam allowances in one direction.

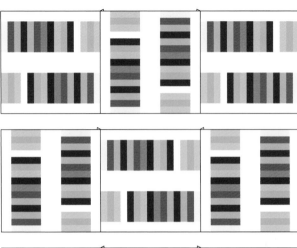

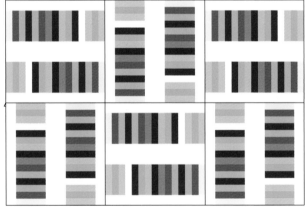

Quilt assembly

2. Sew the cream 5½" x 63" side border strips to the quilt and trim any extra length. Add the cream 5½" x 58" top and bottom border strips in the same way.

Quilting and Finishing

For more information on quilting and finishing your quilt, refer to "Basic Quiltmaking Lessons" on page 74.

1. Make a full-sized template using the pattern for the half orange peel on page 18. Mark the orange peel quilting design in the blocks as shown. Layer and baste together the backing, batting, and quilt top.

2. Quilt the marked lines, connecting the motifs with loops as shown. Quilt two rows of random loops in the border.

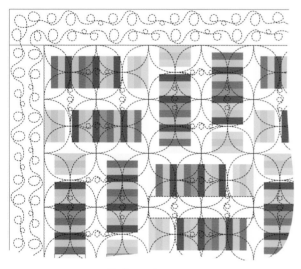

Quilting placement

3. Bind the quilt using the blue 2¼"-wide strips.

Color Option

Sewing with these sumptuous hues was an absolute luxury. I enjoyed seeing what each color looked like next to its neighbors. The gray fabric made a perfect backdrop, allowing the brighter colors and graphic prints to stand out beautifully.

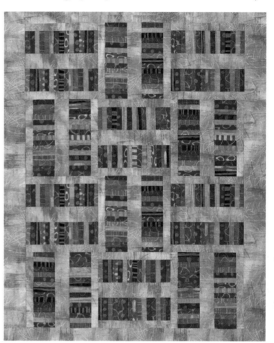

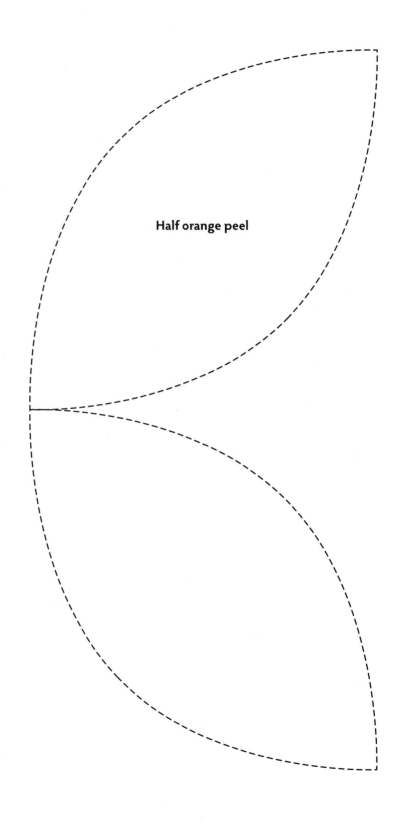

Half orange peel

This is a scrap-tacular quilt to help you bust that stash! Small amounts of many fabrics were stitched into these blocks, adding up to a very pleasing quilt. Originally published in the March/April 1999 issue of *Quiltmaker* (No. 66), "Prairie Schooner" has delighted scrap quilters ever since.

Materials

Yardage is based on 42"-wide fabric.

132 scraps, 4" x 9" *each* of assorted light prints for blocks

132 scraps, 4" x 10" *each* of assorted medium/dark #1 prints for blocks

33 scraps, 8" x 8" *each* of assorted medium/dark #2 prints for blocks

66 scraps, 10" x 10" *each* of assorted medium/dark #3 prints for blocks

5½"-wide strips of black prints to total 400" for border*

⅞ yard of black print for binding

9⅜ yards of fabric for backing

106" x 114" piece of batting

*The strips can measure anywhere from 4" to 18" long.

Cutting

From *each* of the 132 assorted light-print scraps, cut:

2 squares, 2⅞" x 2⅞"
1 square, 2½" x 2½"

From *each* of the 132 assorted medium/dark print #1 scraps, cut:

3 squares, 2⅞" x 2⅞"; cut *1 square* in half diagonally to yield 2 triangles

From *each* of the 33 assorted medium/dark print #2 scraps, cut:

1 square, 6⅞" x 6⅞"; cut into quarters diagonally to yield 4 triangles

From *each* of the 66 assorted medium/dark print #3 scraps, cut:

1 square, 8⅞" x 8⅞"; cut in half diagonally to yield 2 triangles

From the black print for binding, cut:

11 strips, 2¼" x 42"

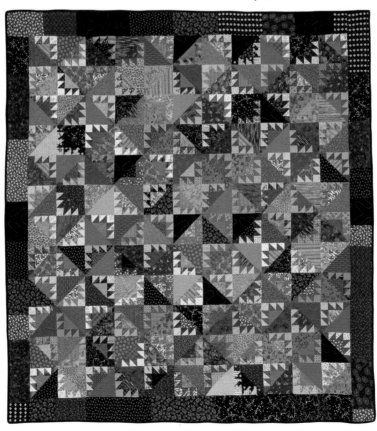

Finished quilt: 98" x 106" | Finished blocks: 8" x 8"

Prairie Schooner

Making the Quilt Center

1. Referring to "Half-Square-Triangle Units" on page 75, pair two matching light 2⅞" squares with two matching medium/dark 2⅞" squares to make four half-square-triangle units.

Make 4.

2. Join two half-square-triangle units and one matching medium/dark 2⅞" triangle. Join two half-square-triangle units, one matching medium/dark 2⅞" triangle, and a matching light 2½" square. Press the seam allowances in the directions shown. Complete the block, sewing the two units just created to one medium/dark 6⅞" triangle and a different medium/dark 8⅞" triangle.

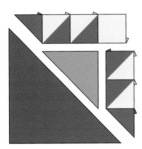

3. Repeat steps 1 and 2 to make 132 blocks.

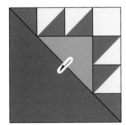

Make 132.

The More, the Merrier

The more colors you include, the more charming this quilt will be. Keep like fabrics together when you cut the scraps to make color placement easier.

4. Arrange the blocks into 12 rows of 11 blocks each, rotating the blocks as shown. Sew the blocks into rows, pressing the seam allowances in opposite directions from row to row. Alternating rows, sew the rows together and press.

Make 6.

Make 6.

Making and Adding the Borders

1. Join the black-print scraps together to make four border strips as follows: 1 strip, 5½" x 91", for the bottom; 1 strip, 5½" x 104", for the left side; 1 strip, 5½" x 96", for the top; and 1 strip, 5½" x 109", for the right side.

2. Beginning with the lower edge of the quilt and working clockwise, sew the border strips to the quilt, trimming the excess length from each strip as needed. Press the seam allowances toward the border.

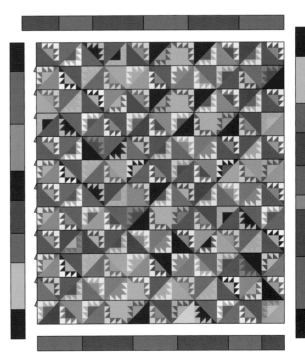

Quilt assembly

Quilting and Finishing

For more information on quilting and finishing your quilt, refer to "Basic Quiltmaking Lessons" on page 74.

1. Layer the backing, batting, and quilt top and baste them together.

2. Quilt a large meandering pattern over the quilt top as shown.

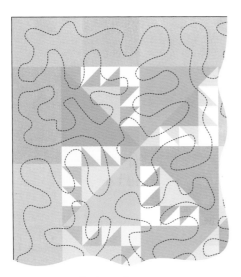

Quilting placement

3. Bind the quilt using the black 2¼"-wide strips.

Color Option

This block is a good one for showcasing stunning prints like these batiks. The two coordinating fabrics used for the small sawtooth triangles illustrate how focus and contrast change when they're placed next to different prints. Since this isn't a scrap quilt, the placement of fabrics in the blocks is planned.

Take a stroll through your fabric collection and gather up scraps to make this quilt, based on an antique version. Paulette named the quilt "Cobblestones" because it reminded her of the square pavers in European cities. She made lots of blocks and dealt them like a deck of cards until she was happy with the arrangement. This timeless pattern was originally published in the May/June 1999 issue of *Quiltmaker* (No. 67).

Materials

Yardage is based on 42"-wide fabric.

4⅝ yards *total* of dark scraps for blocks

3½ yards *total* of light scraps for blocks

2 yards of brown tone-on-tone fabric for setting squares and triangles

¾ yard of gray print for binding

8¼ yards of fabric for backing

93" x 107" piece of batting

Cutting

From the light scraps, cut:

168 squares, 2½" x 2½"

198 rectangles, 2" x 2½"*

198 rectangles, 2" x 5½"*

From the dark scraps, cut:

99 squares, 2½" x 2½"

336 rectangles, 2" x 2½"*

336 rectangles, 2" x 5½"*

From the brown tone-on-tone fabric, cut:

44 squares, 5½" x 5½"

12 squares, 8⅜" x 8⅜"; cut into quarters diagonally to yield 48 triangles

2 squares, 4½" x 4½"; cut in half diagonally to yield 4 triangles

From the gray print, cut:

10 strips, 2¼" x 42"

Cut the rectangles in matching sets of four (two of each size) for each block.

Finished quilt: 85" x 99" | **Finished blocks:** 5" x 5"

Making the Blocks

1. Choose a light 2½" square and a matching set of two each of dark 2" x 2½" and 2" x 5½" rectangles.

2. Sew the 2" x 2½" rectangles to opposite sides of the 2½" square and press the seam allowances away from the square. Sew the 2" x 5½" rectangles to the remaining sides and press to make a dark block.

3. Repeat steps 1 and 2 to make 168 dark blocks. Repeat the steps using a darker center square and lighter rectangles to make 99 light blocks.

Make 168.

Make 99.

Assembling the Quilt

1. Referring to the assembly diagram, arrange the blocks, setting squares, and setting triangles in diagonal rows. Alternate the dark blocks and light blocks, beginning and ending each diagonal row with a dark block.

2. Sew the blocks together into rows and press the seam allowances toward the dark blocks.

3. Sew the rows together and add the corner triangles last. Press.

Add Interest

For added interest, make some blocks either primarily light or primarily dark. This will also increase the scrappy nature of the quilt and make it appear less controlled. Many antique quilts have a great deal of variation in value from block to block.

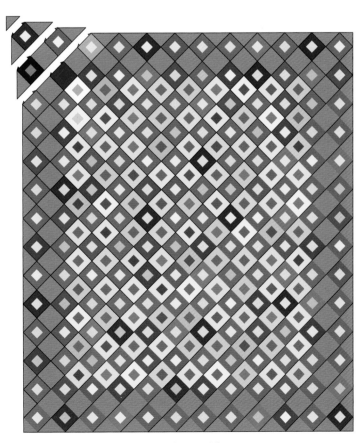

Quilt assembly

Quilting and Finishing

For more information on quilting and finishing your quilt, refer to "Basic Quiltmaking Lessons" on page 74.

1. Layer and baste together the backing, batting, and quilt top.

2. Quilt straight lines through the blocks and setting triangles as shown.

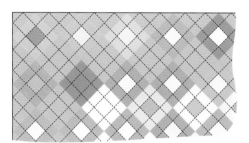

Quilting placement

3. Bind the quilt using the gray 2¼"-wide strips.

Color Option

Using homespun fabrics with batiks creates a cozy textural treasure. A simple layout option is to arrange the blocks in horizontal rows without using any setting squares or triangles.

Delicate and delightful, this quilt was designed around the softly colored and cheerful prints. Colleen and Chloe, partners in the company Toadusew, know quilters love projects that can be made in a day or two. They incorporated a lot of strip piecing—great for beginners or anyone looking for a quick gift.

Materials

Yardage is based on 42"-wide fabric.

2 yards of light-blue print for outer border

1 yard of dark-blue print for inner border and binding

¾ yard of medium-blue tone-on-tone print for sashing

⅝ yard of medium-purple tone-on-tone print for Square-in-a-Square blocks

⅝ yard of teal tone-on-tone print #1 for sashing

⅝ yard of purple tone-on-tone print for sashing

½ yard of medium-purple print for Nine Patch blocks

½ yard of medium-teal tone-on-tone print for Square-in-a-Square blocks

½ yard of teal tone-on-tone print #2 for sashing

⅜ yard of pale-lavender tone-on-tone print for Nine Patch blocks

¼ yard of pale-teal floral for Square-in-a-Square blocks

¼ yard of purple floral for Square-in-a-Square blocks

4½ yards of fabric for backing

72" x 72" piece of batting

Finished throw: 64" x 64" | **Finished blocks:** 6" x 6" and 10" x 10"

Cutting

From the medium-purple print, cut:
  5 strips, 2½" x 42"

From the pale-lavender tone-on-tone print, cut:
  4 strips, 2½" x 42"

From the teal tone-on-tone print #1, cut:
  7 strips, 2½" x 42"

From the medium-blue tone-on-tone print, cut:
  9 strips, 2½" x 42"

From the teal tone-on-tone print #2, cut:
  5 strips, 2½" x 42"

From the purple tone-on-tone print , cut:
  6 strips, 2½" x 42"

From the pale-teal floral, cut:
  5 squares, 6½" x 6½"

From the medium-purple tone-on-tone print, cut:
  10 rectangles, 2½" x 6½"
  10 rectangles, 2½" x 10½"

From the purple floral, cut:
  4 squares, 6½" x 6½"

From the medium-teal tone-on-tone print, cut:
  8 rectangles, 2½" x 6½"
  8 rectangles, 2½" x 10½"

From the dark-blue print, cut:
  6 strips, 1½" x 42"
  7 strips, 2¼" x 42"

From the light-blue print for outer border, cut *on the lengthwise grain:*
  2 strips, 4½" x 59"
  2 strips, 4½" x 67"

Making the Blocks and Sashing

Press the seam allowances in the directions shown in the diagrams.

1. Sew together the medium-purple and pale-lavender 2½" x 42" strips as shown to make two of strip set A and one of strip set B. Cut the strip sets at 2½" intervals to make 32 segments from strip set A and 16 segments from strip set B.

Strip set A.
Make 2.
Cut 32 segments.

Strip set B.
Make 1.
Cut 16 segments.

2. Sew the segments together as shown to make 16 Nine Patch blocks.

Make 16.

3. Sew together 2½" x 42" strips of teal tone-on-tone #1, medium-blue tone-on-tone, and teal tone-on-tone #2 as shown to make three of strip set C. Cut the strip sets at 10½" intervals to make eight sashing units.

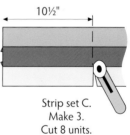

Strip set C.
Make 3.
Cut 8 units.

4. Sew together 2½" x 42" strips of teal tone-on-tone #2, medium-blue tone-on-tone, and purple tone-on-tone as shown to make two of strip set D. Cut the strip sets at 10½" intervals to make four sashing units.

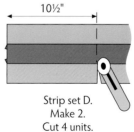

Strip set D.
Make 2.
Cut 4 units.

5. Sew together 2½" x 42" strips of teal tone-on-tone #1, medium-blue tone-on-tone, and purple tone-on-tone as shown to make four of strip set E. Cut the strip sets at 10½" intervals to make 12 sashing units.

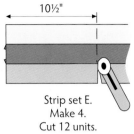

10½"

Strip set E.
Make 4.
Cut 12 units.

6. Sew the pale-teal and purple-floral 6½" squares together with medium-purple rectangles and medium-teal rectangles as shown to make five pale-teal floral and four purple-floral Square-in-a-Square blocks.

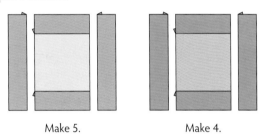

Make 5.   Make 4.

Assembling the Quilt Top

1. Join the blocks and sashing units as shown to make the rows and press the seam allowances toward the sashing units. Sew the rows together and press.

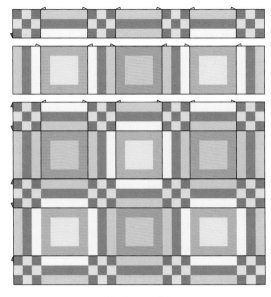

Quilt assembly

2. Sew the dark-blue 1½"-wide inner-border strips together and cut two lengths of 57" for the sides and two lengths of 59" for the top and bottom. Sew the 57" strips to the sides of the quilt and trim any extra length. Add the top and bottom strips to the top and bottom of the quilt in the same way. Press the seam allowances toward the border.

3. Add the light-blue 4½" x 59" outer-border strips to the sides and the 4½" x 67" strips to the top and bottom of the quilt. Trim the extra length and press the seam allowances toward the outer border.

Quilting and Finishing

For more information on quilting and finishing your quilt, refer to "Basic Quiltmaking Lessons" on page 74.

1. Layer and baste together the backing, batting, and quilt top.

2. Quilt the cotton sprig quilting design over the quilt surface.

Quilting placement

3. Bind the quilt using the dark-blue 2¼"-wide strips.

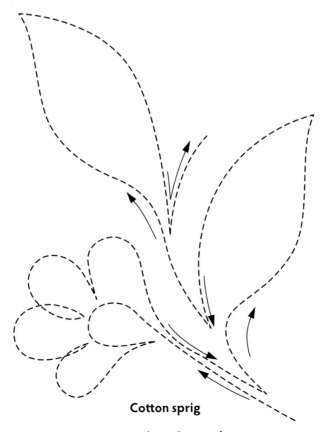

Cotton sprig

Arrows indicate direction for
continuous-line machine quilting.

Designed by Barbara Lebbing; sewn by Diane Harris; quilted by J. Renée Howell

Classic colors star in a reproduction beauty. Sometimes it's a nice surprise when you switch up the details of a design just to see what will happen. This is a variation of a traditional Robbing Peter to Pay Paul block, using straight lines in place of the curves. This scrappy quilt of reproduction blues, blacks, reds, and shirtings is made from one block, with the value placement reversed. It's helpful to remember that value is relative—a fabric that appears dark in one setting will seem lighter in another. A wide range of values keeps things interesting in this simple design.

Materials

Yardage is based on 42"-wide fabric; fat quarters measure approximately 18" x 21".

- 9 yards *total* or 36 fat quarters of assorted light prints for blocks
- 9 yards *total* or 36 fat quarters of assorted dark prints for blocks
- 3½ yards of black print for outer border and binding
- 1 yard of red print for inner border
- 10½ yards of fabric for backing
- 119" x 119" piece of batting

Cutting

From the red print, cut:
10 strips, 2½" x 42"

From the black print, cut *on the lengthwise grain:*
2 strips, 6½" x 101"
2 strips, 6½" x 113"
5 binding strips, 2¼" x 93"

Finished quilt: 110½" x 110½" | **Finished blocks:** 10½" x 10½"

Making the Blocks

1. Make 324 paper copies of the foundation pattern on page 36.

2. Choose two light 2½" x 6½" rectangles and one dark square. Place a square on the foundation right side up, covering the space marked 1. Place a rectangle on the foundation wrong side up, along the edge of the space marked 2 so that the raw edge is parallel to the line on the foundation between space 1 and 2. Hold the foundation up to the light to make sure you'll have a ¼" seam allowance. Pin in place. With the paper side up, stitch along the line between 1 and 2 using a shorter-than-normal stitch length. Trim the seam allowances to ¼" and press. Trim the excess fabric even with the outer edge of the foundation. Repeat to add the second rectangle over space 3. Trim the edges of the block even with the foundation.

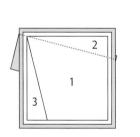

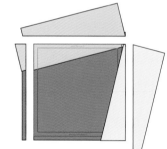

3. Repeat step 2 to make a total of 164 dark units.

Make 164.

4. Using one light square and two dark rectangles, make a light unit in the same manner as in step 2. Make 160 light units.

Make 160.

5. Sew four dark units together as shown to make block A. Make 41 of block A. Sew four light units together to make block B. Make 40 of block B.

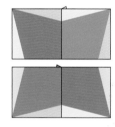

Block A.
Make 41.

Block B.
Make 40.

Assembling the Quilt

1. Arrange the blocks in nine rows of nine blocks each, beginning the first row with block A and alternating with block B. Press the seam allowances in opposite directions from row to row. Join the blocks into rows, and then sew the rows together. Press.

Quilt assembly

2. Carefully remove the foundation papers.

3. Sew the red-print 2½"-wide strips together into one long strip. Cut this strip into two lengths of 97" for the side inner border and two lengths of 101" for the top and bottom inner border. Sew the side strips to the quilt and trim any extra length. Press the seam allowances toward the border just added. Repeat for the top and bottom strips. Add the outer border in the same way.

Quilting and Finishing

For more information on quilting and finishing your quilt, refer to "Basic Quiltmaking Lessons" on page 74.

1. Mark the desired quilting design over the surface of the quilt.

2. Layer and baste together the backing, batting, and quilt top.

3. Quilt the marked motifs. The circular quilting design used on the quilt shown illustrates a style often found on antique quilts, in which the quilting pattern largely ignores the lines of piecing and instead creates another design element. When you choose a pattern for quilting that does not integrate with the piecing, it may be simpler to mark the quilt back, and then to quilt from the back.

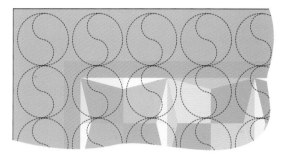

Quilting placement

4. Bind the quilt using the black 2¼"-wide strips.

Color Option

Using just two fabrics sets a serene mood. The contemporary print in earthy colors is an interesting juxtaposition.

¼" seam allowance

2

1

3

Foundation pattern

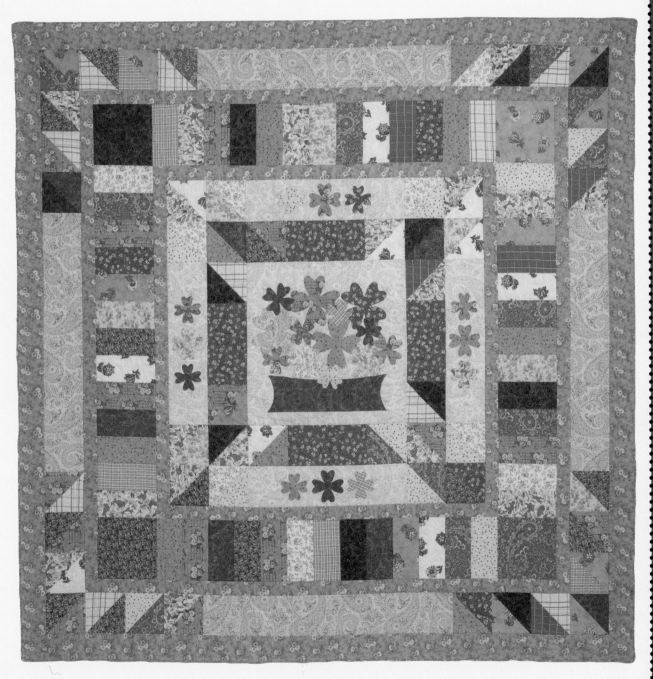

No spring showers are needed to grow these flowers! Wendy loves to incorporate primary colors in home decorating, and she wanted a design that was cheerful and full of life. Flowers were a natural choice. The large pieces in this quilt are perfect for showcasing fabulous prints.

Materials

Yardage is based on 42"-wide fabric.

5⅓ yards *total* of assorted medium and tone-on-tone prints for flowers and borders*

3⅔ yards of blue print for border 3, border 5, border 7, and binding

1⅝ yards of cream print for center block and border 2

⅞ yard of gold print for border 6

½ yard of red print for border 1

¼ yard of red tone-on-tone print for basket

9⅛ yards of fabric for backing

102" x 102" piece of batting

1¾ yards of 18"-wide fusible web

Tear-away stabilizer

*Wendy used 16 prints, ⅓- to ½-yard cuts of each.

Finished quilt: 94" x 94" | **Finished center block:** 24" x 24"

Cutting

The appliqué patterns are on pages 42 and 43. Read "Appliquéing the Blocks" below before cutting your appliqués.

From the cream print, cut:
   1 square, 25½" x 25½"
   4 rectangles, 7½" x 25½"

From the red tone-on-tone print, cut:
   1 basket

From the assorted medium and tone-on-tone prints*, cut *a total of:*
   4 of flower A
   2 of flower B
   6 of flower C
   13 of flower D
   52 squares, 6⅞" x 6⅞"
   52 rectangles, 4½" x 9½"
   4 squares, 9½" x 9½"

From the red print, cut:
   4 rectangles, 6½" x 12½"

From the gold print, cut:
   4 rectangles, 6½" x 38½"

From the blue print, cut *on the lengthwise grain:*
   2 strips, 2½" x 48½"
   2 strips, 2½" x 52½"
   2 strips, 2½" x 70½"
   2 strips, 2½" x 74½"
   2 strips, 4½" x 89"
   2 strips, 4½" x 97"

From the remainder of the blue print, cut:
   10 strips, 2¼" x 42"

*You can also cut some of these pieces from leftover red print and red tone-on-tone print.

Appliquéing the Blocks

1. Trace the basket and flowers A, B, C, and D onto the paper side of the fusible web, leaving at least ½" between the pieces. Cut just outside of the lines.

2. Following the manufacturer's instructions, iron the web, paper side up, to the wrong side of your chosen fabrics. Cut out the shapes exactly on the drawn lines. Carefully pull away the paper backing. Fuse the pieces to the cream print 25½" square as shown in the diagram or in an arrangement pleasing to you. You can finger-press the background fabric in half lengthwise, crosswise, and diagonally to establish placement guidelines for the appliqué pieces if desired.

> ### Eliminate Stiffness
>
> For pieces larger than 1", such as the basket, you can cut out the center of the fusible web ¼" to ½" *inside* the drawn line, making a ring of fusible web.

3. Using a tear-away stabilizer on the back and thread to blend, machine blanket-stitch around the appliqués. Gently remove the stabilizer.

Machine blanket stitch

4. With the design centered, trim the block to 24½" x 24½".

5. Appliqué the C and D flowers to the cream print 7½" x 25½" background rectangles in the same manner. Trim the rectangles to 6½" x 24½".

Make 4.

Piecing the Borders

Press the seam allowances in the direction indicated by the arrows in the diagrams.

1. Referring to "Half-Square-Triangle Units" on page 75, randomly pair 6⅞" squares of different fabrics to make 52 half-square-triangle units.

Make 52.

2. Referring to the assembly diagram below, join two half-square-triangle units and one red-print 6½" x 12½" rectangle to make border 1. Make two for the sides. Join four half-square-triangle units and one red-print rectangle for the top and bottom; make two.

3. To make border 2, join two half-square-triangle units and the appliquéd rectangle as shown. Make two for the sides. Join four half-square-triangle units and the appliquéd rectangle for the top and bottom; make two.

4. Randomly join 13 assorted 4½" x 9½" rectangles to make each border 4 strip. Add assorted 9½" squares to both ends of two of these strips to make the top and bottom border strips.

5. Sew together the remaining half-square-triangle units and the gold-print 6½" x 38½" strips as shown below to make border 6.

Assembling the Quilt Top

1. Matching centers and ends, sew border 1 side strips to the basket appliqué block. Repeat to add the border 1 top and bottom strips.

2. Add borders 2–6 in the same way, using the blue-print 2½"-wide strips for borders 3 and 5. Always add the shorter border strips to the sides first, and then add the longer strips to the top and bottom.

3. Sew the blue-print 4½"-wide border 7 side strips to the quilt and trim any extra length. Repeat to add the border 7 top and bottom strips.

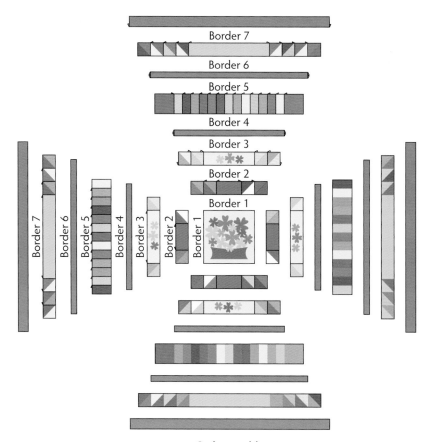

Quilt assembly

Quilting and Finishing

For more information on quilting and finishing your quilt, refer to "Basic Quiltmaking Lessons" on page 74.

1. Layer and baste together the backing, batting, and quilt top.

2. Quilt in the ditch around the appliquéd flowers and basket. Quilt parallel lines in the basket 1½" apart. Outline quilt the appliqué as shown. Use the appliquéd flowers as guides to quilt flowers in the borders, echo quilting some of the flowers as shown to travel between flowers.

Quilting placement

3. Bind the quilt using the blue 2¼"-wide strips.

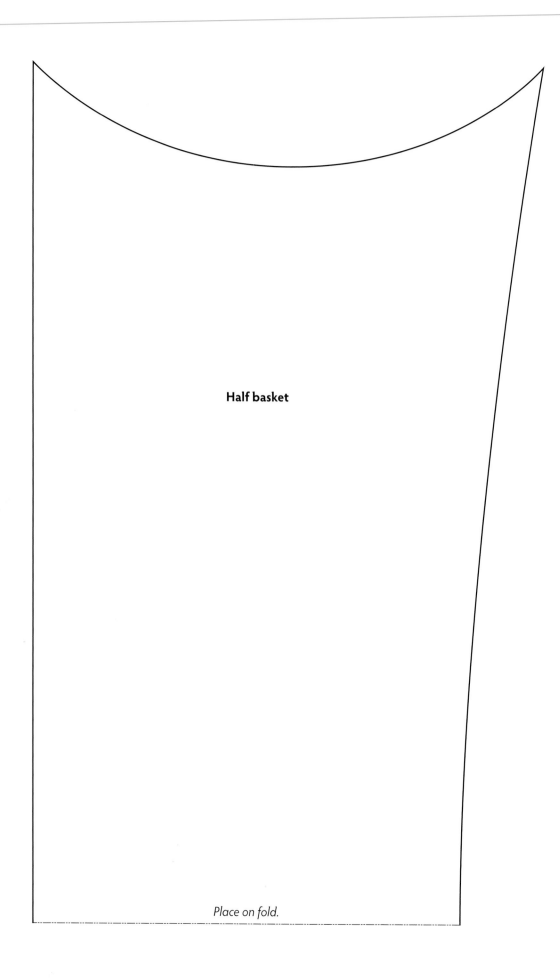

Half basket

Place on fold.

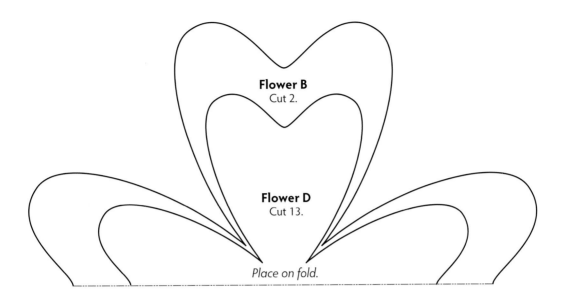

Flower B
Cut 2.

Flower D
Cut 13.

Place on fold.

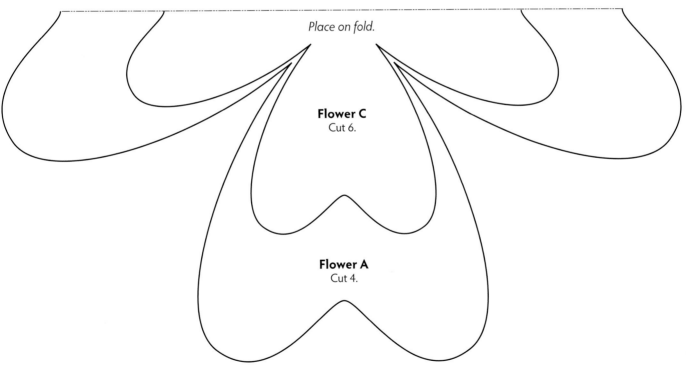

Place on fold.

Flower C
Cut 6.

Flower A
Cut 4.

Designed and made by Amanda Murphy; quilted by Janice Hayes

Snuggle up with something warm. Amanda's collection of lovely chocolate-brown fabrics inspired this design. The rich browns and cool blues play well together. This quilt is easier to sew than it looks. It's assembled in vertical rows rather than as blocks in horizontal rows. Amanda used eight different fabrics, including the blue border fabric; simply use more fabrics if you prefer a scrappier quilt.

Materials

Yardage is based on 42"-wide fabric.

2½ yards of blue print for border 3 and binding
2¼ yards *total* of assorted prints for rows
2 yards of dark-brown print for rows
1⅜ yards of cream print for rows and border 2
½ yard of gold print for border 1
5¾ yards of fabric for backing
72" x 96" piece of batting

Cutting

From the cream print, cut:
17 strips, 1¾" x 42"
8 strips, 1¼" x 42"
14 rectangles, 1½" x 1¾"

From the dark-brown print, cut:
8 strips, 4¼" x 42"
18 strips, 1½" x 42"
28 rectangles, 1½" x 3¼"

From the assorted prints, cut:
98 rectangles, 3½" x 7¼"
12 rectangles, 2¼" x 3½"

From the gold print, cut:
7 strips, 1¾" x 42"

From the blue print, cut *on the lengthwise grain:*
2 strips, 3¾" x 84"
2 strips, 3¾" x 66"
4 binding strips, 2¼" x 80"

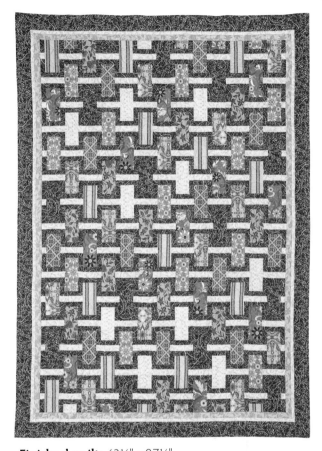

Finished quilt: 63½" x 87¼"

Making the Quilt Center

Press the seam allowances in the directions shown in the diagrams.

1. Join two cream 1¾" x 42" strips and two dark-brown 4¼"-wide strips as shown to make strip set A. Make four strip sets. Cut the strip sets at 1½" intervals to make 98 segments as shown.

Strip set A.
Make 4.
Cut 98 segments.

2. Join one cream 1¾" x 42" strip and two dark-brown 1½" x 42" strips as shown to make strip set B. Make nine strip sets. Cut the strip sets at 3½" intervals to make 97 segments.

Strip set B.
Make 9.
Cut 97 segments.

3. To make row 1, join two dark-brown 1½" x 3¼" rectangles, one cream-print 1½" x 1¾" rectangle, and seven segments from step 1 as shown at right. Make 14 rows.

4. To make row 2, join eight assorted 3½" x 7¼" rectangles and seven segments from step 2 as shown. Make seven rows.

5. To make row 3, join two assorted 2¼" x 3½" rectangles, eight segments from step 2, and seven assorted 3½" x 7¼" rectangles as shown. Make six rows.

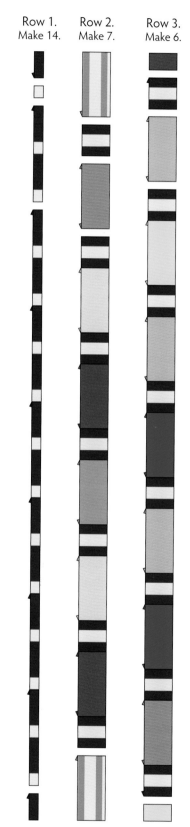

Row 1.
Make 14.

Row 2.
Make 7.

Row 3.
Make 6.

6. Matching seam lines, sew the rows together as shown in the quilt assembly diagram. Press the seam allowances toward rows 2 and 3.

Quilt assembly

Adding the Borders

1. Sew the gold-print 1¾" x 42" strips together for border 1. Cut two lengths of 80" for the sides and two lengths of 58" for the top and bottom. Sew the strips to the sides of the quilt and trim any extra length. Press the seam allowances toward the border just added. Add the top and bottom strips to the top and bottom of the quilt in the same way.

2. Sew the cream-print 1¼" x 42" strips together for border 2. Cut two lengths of 82" for the sides and two lengths of 60" for the top and bottom. Sew the border 2 strips to the quilt in the same way as border 1.

3. Add the blue-print 3¾" x 84" strips to the sides of the quilt and press. Trim any extra length. Add the blue-print 3¾" x 66" strips to the top and bottom. Press.

Quilting and Finishing

For more information on quilting and finishing your quilt, refer to "Basic Quiltmaking Lessons" on page 74.

1. Mark the quilting designs as desired. The quilt shown was quilted with leafy vines and tendrils as shown in the quilting placement diagram.

2. Layer and baste together the backing, batting, and quilt top.

3. Quilt the marked motifs. Quilt borders 1 and 2 in the ditch.

Quilting placement

4. Bind the quilt using the blue 2¼"-wide strips.

Color Option

In this alternate colorway, the red and cream fabrics make a perfect backdrop to showcase all of the wonderful patterns and colors of the print fabrics.

Happy to Be Scrappy

Designed and made by Leslie Pearce

48

This simple but striking pattern first appeared in the September/October 1999 issue of *Quiltmaker* (No. 69). Since then, the magazine staff has received numerous photographs of readers' versions, and they hope to see even more of this appealing quilt. The quilt is made up of two traditional and easy-to-piece blocks—the Nine Patch and the Split Nine Patch.

Materials

Yardage is based on 42"-wide fabric.

7 yards *total* of assorted dark scraps for blocks and binding

4 yards *total* of assorted cream scraps for blocks

8⅔ yards of fabric for backing

98" x 98" piece of batting

Cutting

From the assorted cream scraps, cut:

396 squares, 3" x 3"*

84 squares, 3⅜" x 3⅜"

From the assorted dark scraps, cut:

732 squares, 3" x 3"*

84 squares, 3⅜" x 3⅜"

10 strips, 2¼" x 42"**

For strip piecing, do not cut the 3" squares; see "Strip-Piecing Shortcuts" on page 50 for this timesaving method.

**To add variety, cut each binding strip from a different dark print.*

Choosing Fabrics

The cream scraps are a mix of small-scale and tone-on-tone prints. The dark scraps are small- and medium-scale prints. Several medium-value scraps have been tossed in to add sparkle and variety. Medium-gray thread is ideal for piecing multicolored patches.

If you don't have a stash of scraps, look for fat quarters (precut fabrics that measure approximately 18" x 21"). You'll need at least 16 cream and 28 dark fat quarters for this quilt.

Finished quilt: 90" x 90" | **Finished blocks:** 7½" x 7½"

Making the Blocks

Press the seam allowances in the directions shown in the diagrams. If you have large scraps on hand or leftover 3"-wide strips, see "Strip-Piecing Shortcuts" below.

1. Referring to "Half-Square-Triangle Units" on page 75, pair the 3⅜" cream squares with medium or dark squares to make 168 half-square-triangle units.

Make 168.

2. Using three cream 3" squares, four dark 3" squares, and two half-square-triangle units from step 1, arrange and sew the Split Nine Patch block as shown. Make a total of 84 blocks.

Make 84.

3. Sew together nine cream 3" squares to make a light Nine Patch block. Make a total of 16 blocks.

Make 16.

4. Sew together nine dark 3" squares to make a dark Nine Patch block. Make a total of 44 blocks.

Make 44.

Strip-Piecing Shortcuts

If you have large scraps or leftover strips, you can save time by strip piecing instead of cutting individual 3" squares. From the cream and dark scraps, cut strips 3" wide.

Split Nine Patch blocks: Join two strips to make strip sets as shown. Cut 84 segments 3" wide from the cream strip sets and 168 segments 3" wide from the dark strip sets.

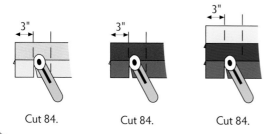

Cut 84.   Cut 84.   Cut 84.

Nine Patch blocks: Join three strips to make strip sets as shown. Cut 48 segments 3" wide from the cream strip sets and 132 segments 3" wide from the dark strip sets.

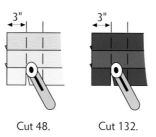

Cut 48.   Cut 132.

Now you have a head start! Refer to "Making the Blocks" and follow steps 1–4 to complete the blocks.

Assembling the Quilt Top

Referring to the assembly diagram, arrange the blocks in 12 rows of 12 blocks each, rotating the Split Nine Patch blocks to create the design. Sew the blocks together to make the rows. Press the seam allowances in opposite directions from row to row. Sew the rows together. Press.

Quilt assembly

Quilting and Finishing

For more information on quilting and finishing your quilt, refer to "Basic Quiltmaking Lessons" on page 74.

1. Layer the backing, batting, and quilt top. Baste the layers together. To personalize your quilt with random, innovative designs like Leslie did, see "Stretching Tradition" on page 52. For a simple quilting option, quilt a grid ¼" in from the seam lines and ½" in from the raw edges.

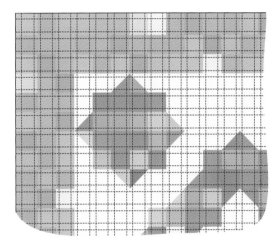

Grid quilting placement

2. Sew the assorted dark-print 2¼"-wide binding strips together to make one long strip. Finish the edges of your quilt with this binding.

Stretching Tradition

Leslie adapted hand-quilting designs so that she could machine quilt "Happy to Be Scrappy" without doing any marking. She expanded the definition of meander quilting (randomly placed curvy quilting) to include designs such as figure eights, swirls, zigzags, and curlicues in the light areas as shown in the photographs. To sew these, drop or cover the feed dogs and attach a darning foot. Before quilting your project, be sure to warm up on a sample quilt sandwich.

For the dark areas in the center of the quilt, Leslie used two different stitching methods. In the diamond rings, she free-motion quilted gentle arcs as shown in the block quilting detail. In the solid diamond shapes, she quilted a diagonal grid of straight lines using a walking foot on her machine. A straight grid was stitched in the Nine Patch blocks making up the border, with stitching lines quilted ¼" from each seam line and ½" from the raw edges.

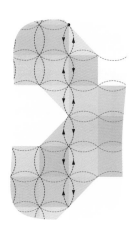

Block quilting detail

Arrows indicate direction for continuous-line machine quilting.

Quilting placement

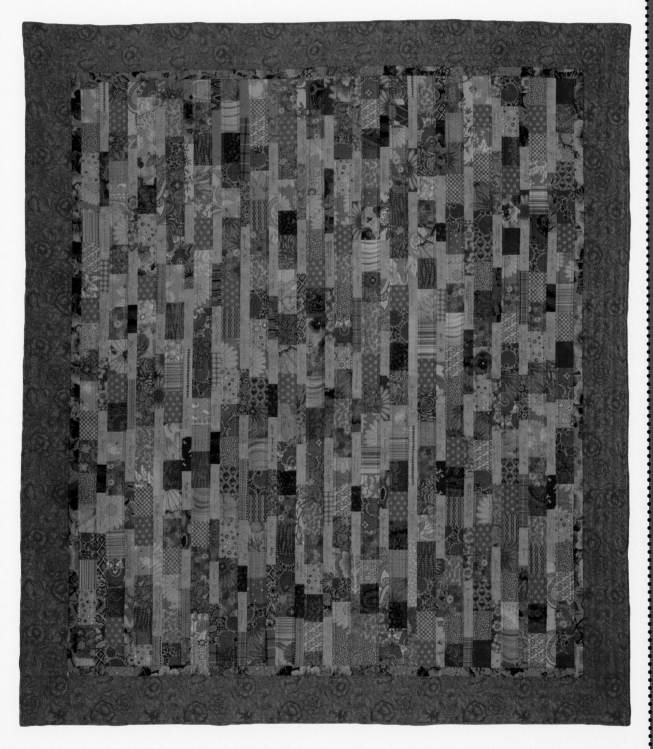

Give new meaning to those best wishes from family and friends with a signature quilt. When Diane's daughter Holly was married, wedding guests signed strips of fabric instead of a guest book. Many people conveyed a lot in the small space they were given, making the quilt a very special keepsake for the young couple.

Materials

Yardage is based on 42"-wide fabric.

2⅔ yards *total* of assorted red, pink, and orange prints for wide rows

2⅛ yards of red print for outer border and binding

⅞ yard of green tone-on-tone print for signature background

¾ yard *total* of assorted green and blue prints for signature rows

½ yard of green print for inner border

4⅜ yards of fabric for backing

73" x 80" piece of batting

Removable marker

Pigma Micron pens (.05 tip)

Freezer paper

Cutting

Before cutting the green tone-on-tone fabric, iron freezer paper to the wrong side to stabilize it for signing.

From the green tone-on-tone print, cut:
85 rectangles, 1½" x 8"*

From the assorted green and blue prints, cut:
140 rectangles, 1½" x 3½" or longer**

From the assorted red, pink, and orange prints, cut:
375 rectangles, 2½" x 3½" or longer**

From the green print, cut:
6 strips, 1½" x 42"

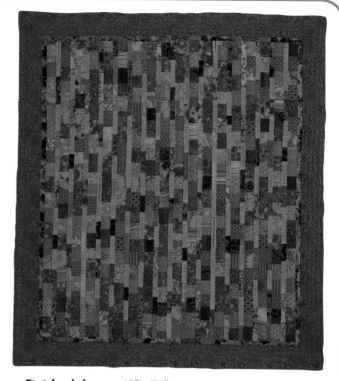

Finished throw: *65" x 72"*

From the red print, cut *on the lengthwise grain:*
2 strips, 5½" x 65"
2 strips, 5½" x 68"
5 binding strips, 2¼" x 60"

It's a good idea to cut several extra rectangles to allow for mistakes made by guests when signing.

**These rectangles can vary in length from 3½" to 5½" or more. The quantity is approximate. You may have extra, or you may need to cut additional rectangles when sewing them into rows.*

Preparing the Signature Rectangles

1. On each green tone-on-tone 1½" x 8" rectangle, clearly outline the area for the signature. Using a removable marker, draw a box approximately ¾" x 7" centered on each rectangle as shown. This allows space between the signature and the seam allowance to give you some extra insurance. (Don't be surprised if a few people still write outside the box.) Test your marker for removability before marking all of the boxes. Diane used a blue wash-out marker.

2. After the rectangles have been signed, gently remove the freezer paper and the marked box around each signature. To remove the wash-out marker, rinse each strip under cold running water. Let strips dry as needed and press gently.

3. Trim each rectangle to the desired length. Diane left a 1" space before and after each signature, and regardless of spacing, she left each signature rectangle at least 4½" long.

Making the Quilt Center

It's helpful to use a design wall when joining the rows.

1. Join signature strips alternately with the assorted green- and blue-print 1½"-wide rectangles to make a row about 63" long. Place longer print rectangles at each end of the row to allow for trimming. Press all seam allowances in one direction. Make 17 rows.

2. Randomly join the assorted red, pink, and orange 2½"-wide rectangles to make a row approximately 63" long. Press all the seam allowances in the opposite direction of the signature rows. Make 18 rows.

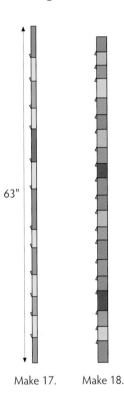

Make 17.   Make 18.

3. Sew the rows together to complete the quilt center, staggering the rows slightly as needed to offset the seams. Press all the seam allowances toward the signature rows. Trim across the top and bottom to make the length 60½".

Quilt assembly

Change Is Good

To keep the quilt top from becoming distorted, alternate sewing directions when joining the rows.

Adding the Borders

1. Join the green-print inner-border strips and cut two strips equal to the length of your quilt center (60½"). Sew these to the quilt sides and trim. Press toward the border just added. Cut two strips for the top and bottom; sew these to the quilt and trim any extra length. Press.

2. Repeat the process to add the red-print outer border.

Color Option

Create a calming mood in this subtler version, appropriate for someone who enjoys a soft, neutral palette.

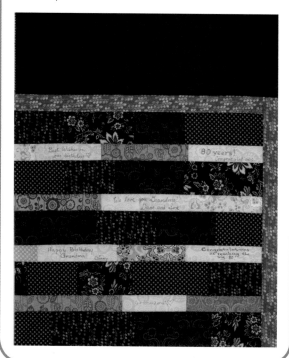

Quilting and Finishing

For more information on quilting and finishing your quilt, refer to "Basic Quiltmaking Lessons" on page 74.

1. Layer and baste together the backing, batting, and quilt top.

2. Referring to the quilting placement diagram, quilt ¼" outside the seam lines that join the rows. Quilt the inner border in the ditch. Add wavy lines of quilting in the outer border.

3. Bind the quilt using the red-print 2½"-wide strips.

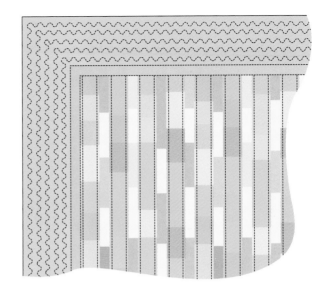

Quilting placement

Too Many Signatures?

If you have many more signatures than will fit on a quilt top, consider putting signatures on both sides of the quilt. Doing so buys you twice as much space and a double-sided quilt!

Making Memories

Follow these tips for a successful keepsake quilt.

- Choose a relatively plain fabric for the signatures. Test the pens you plan to use on the actual fabric for visibility and bleeding.

- Prewashing the signature fabric is a personal choice. The inked signatures may soak into the fabric better if the sizing has been washed away, but if you wash the signature fabric, you should wash all of the other fabrics as well.

- A note about seam allowances: it's very important that you clearly outline the area into which the signature goes.

- Test for removability before marking the boxes. Diane used a blue wash-out marker and rinsed each strip under cold running water after the strips were signed.

- Give guests a chance to "warm up" before signing. Iron a few 8" x 8" pieces of the signature fabric to freezer paper and mark them boldly, "PRACTICE HERE."

- The instructions given when the strips are signed must be very clear and in writing (e.g., on a small sign). Here's an example: Using one of the pens provided, please sign your name on a green rectangle by writing inside the blue box. Do a trial run on the large practice piece.

- Use Pigma Micron pens; size .05 works best.

- Diane left it up to the guests as to how they wanted to sign, for example, as a family or individually, or whether they wanted to sign their legal names ("John Volk") or family names ("Grandpa John"). Several parents allowed young children to sign and one mom signed on her baby's behalf. Diane had guests who chose each of these options and it all worked out.

- If possible, post someone who is familiar with the process near the signing area to answer any questions.

- Consider when you will have the signing take place. Not wanting to create a bottleneck before the ceremony, Diane opted to use a table at the reception instead. Most people signed as they arrived at the reception, but before guests left, Diane reminded people to sign if they hadn't yet done so. One guest asked if she could take a rectangle home for others to sign; she mailed it back promptly.

- Keep in mind that you're not creating a masterpiece quilt, but an irreplaceable keepsake from a special time with family and friends. Wedding guests will leave behind thoughts and sentiments to be cherished for a lifetime.

Julie loves mixing and matching shapes and colors to come up with something fresh and new. This medallion quilt combines the look of an on-point and a straight setting, but it's pieced in horizontal rows. The result is acres of sunny yellow next to refreshing blues. It's fast and bold—packing a lot of punch with limited piecing.

Materials

Yardage is based on 42"-wide fabric.

3 yards of light-blue floral for blocks and outer border

2½ yards of dark-blue tone-on-tone print for blocks and pieced border

2 yards of yellow print for blocks and pieced border

1¼ yards of light-blue tone-on-tone print #1 for blocks and binding

1⅛ yards *each* of blue plaid and yellow-and-blue plaid for blocks and pieced border

1 yard of pale-blue tone-on-tone print for blocks

⅝ yard of medium-blue tone-on-tone print #1 for blocks

⅝ yard of light-blue tone-on-tone print #2 for blocks

½ yard of medium-blue tone-on-tone print #2 for blocks

½ yard of cream-and-blue floral for blocks

⅜ yard of light blue-and-cream floral for blocks

⅜ yard of medium blue-and-cream floral for blocks

11" x 11" piece of light-yellow tone-on-tone print for center block

9¼ yards of fabric for backing

104" x 104" piece of batting

Finished quilt: 96" x 96" | Finished blocks: 12" x 12"

Cutting

From the yellow print, cut:
12 squares, 6⅞" x 6⅞" cut in half diagonally to yield 24 triangles
4 rectangles, 12½" x 24½"

From each of the blue plaid and yellow-and-blue plaid, cut:
2 squares, 6⅞" x 6⅞" cut in half diagonally to yield 4 triangles
4 rectangles, 6½" x 33½"

From the pale-blue tone-on-tone print, cut:
8 squares, 6⅞" x 6⅞" cut in half diagonally to yield 16 triangles
1 square, 13¼" x 13¼" cut into quarters diagonally to yield 4 triangles
24 squares, 2½" x 2½"
4 rectangles, 2½" x 4½"

From the medium blue-and-cream floral, cut:
16 squares, 3½" x 3½"

From the light blue-and-cream floral, cut:
16 squares, 3½" x 3½"

From the cream-and-blue floral, cut:
32 squares, 3½" x 3½"

From the medium-blue tone-on-tone print #2, cut:
2 squares, 12½" x 12½"

From the dark-blue tone-on-tone print, cut *on the lengthwise grain*:
8 strips, 6½" x 44½"

From the remainder of the dark-blue tone-on-tone print, cut:
1 square, 13¼" x 13¼" cut into quarters diagonally to yield 4 triangles
8 squares, 6½" x 6½"

From the medium-blue tone-on-tone print #1, cut:
2 squares, 12½" x 12½"
16 squares, 2½" x 2½"
4 squares, 4½" x 4½"

From the light-blue floral, cut *on the lengthwise grain*:
4 strips, 6½" x 100" for pieced border

From the remainder of the light-blue floral, cut:
2 squares, 12½" x 12½"

From the light blue tone-on-tone print #2, cut:
2 squares, 6⅞" x 6⅞" cut in half diagonally to yield 4 triangles
8 squares, 2½" x 2½"
12 rectangles, 2½" x 4½"
4 rectangles, 4½" x 12½"

From the light-blue tone-on-tone print #1, cut:
2 squares, 12½" x 12½"
10 strips, 2¼" x 42"

From the light-yellow tone-on-tone print, cut:
1 square, 9" x 9"

Making the Quilt Center

Press the seam allowances in the directions shown in the diagrams.

1. Using two yellow-print, one blue-plaid, and one pale-blue tone-on-tone 6⅞" triangle, make two half-square-triangle units as shown. Make two four-patch units using two medium blue-and-cream floral, two light blue-and-cream floral, and four cream-and-blue floral 3½" squares. Join the units to make block A. Make four of block A.

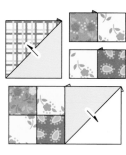

Block A.
Make 4.

2. Using two yellow-print, one yellow-and-blue plaid, and one pale-blue tone-on-tone 6⅞" triangle, make two half-square-triangle units as shown. Make two four-patch units using two medium blue-and-cream floral, two light blue-and-cream floral, and four cream-and-blue floral 3½" squares. Join the units to make block B. Make four blocks.

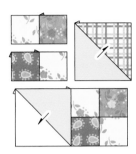

Block B.
Make 4.

3. Join two yellow-print 6⅞" triangles to one pale-blue tone-on-tone quarter-square triangle from the 13¼" square as shown to make a flying-geese unit. Make a second unit using two pale-blue tone-on-tone 6⅞" triangles and one dark-blue tone-on-tone quarter-square triangle from the 13¼" square. Join the units to make block C. Make four blocks.

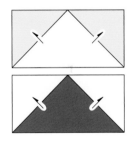

Block C.
Make 4.

4. Make units as shown, using the following patches:

- 2 light-blue tone-on-tone #1 squares, 2½" x 2½"
- 4 medium-blue tone-on-tone #1 squares, 2½" x 2½"
- 6 pale-blue tone-on-tone squares, 2½" x 2½"
- 3 light-blue tone-on-tone #2 rectangles, 2½" x 4½"
- 1 pale-blue tone-on-tone rectangle, 2½" x 4½"

Sew the units together with one medium-blue tone-on-tone #1 square, 4½" x 4½", and one light-blue tone-on-tone #2 rectangle, 4½" x 12½", as shown above right.

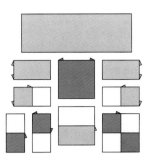

5. Align a dark-blue tone-on-tone 6½" square on the upper-left corner of the unit from step 4 with right sides together, as shown. Draw a diagonal line from corner to corner on the square and sew on the marked line. Trim the seam allowances to ¼", flip the patch open, and press. Repeat with a second dark-blue square in the upper-right corner. This completes block D. Make four blocks.

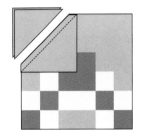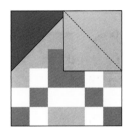

Block D.
Make 4.

6. Join light-blue tone-on-tone #2 triangles to each side of the light-yellow tone-on-tone 9" square to make block E.

Block E.
Make 1.

7. Join the blocks and squares into rows as shown in the assembly diagram below. You'll use two 12½" squares *each* of light-blue tone-on-tone #1, medium-blue tone-on-tone #1, medium-blue tone-on-tone #2, and light-blue floral. Sew the rows together.

Quilt assembly

Adding the Borders

Press the seam allowances in the directions shown in the diagrams.

1. Matching the centers, join each of the blue-plaid 6½" x 33½" strips to a dark-blue tone-on-tone 6½" x 44½" strip as shown to make a border 1 unit. Make four.

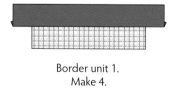

Border unit 1.
Make 4.

2. Repeat step 1 using a yellow-and-blue plaid 6½" x 33½" strip and dark-blue tone-on-tone 6½" x 44½" strip to make border 2 unit. Make four.

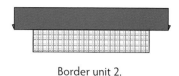

Border unit 2.
Make 4.

3. Join a border 1 unit to a yellow-print 12½" x 24½" rectangle using the stitch-and-flip technique. Align the border 1 unit on the left side of the rectangle with right sides together. Draw a 45° diagonal line on the border, pin, and sew on the marked line. Trim the seam allowances to ¼", flip the border unit open, and press.

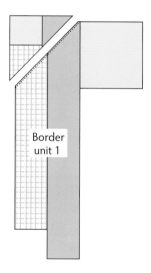

Border
unit 1

4. Sew a border 2 unit to the right side of the unit from step 3 using the same technique.

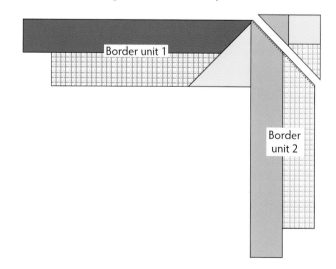

Border unit 1

Border
unit 2

5. Repeat steps 3 and 4 to make four borders.

Border section.
Make 4.

6. Sew a light-blue-floral 6½" x 100" strip to each of the four borders from step 5, matching the centers.

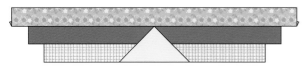

Border.
Make 4.

7. Sew the border strips to the quilt, matching the centers; start and stop ¼" from the edges of the quilt and backstitch. Miter the corners, referring to "Mitered Borders" on page 76. Trim the seam allowances to ¼" and press them open.

Quilting and Finishing

For more information on quilting and finishing your quilt, refer to "Basic Quiltmaking Lessons" on page 74.

1. Layer and baste together the backing, batting, and quilt top.

2. Quilt the "Loopy Swirl" quilting design on page 64 over the quilt surface.

Quilting placement

3. Bind the quilt using the light-blue tone-on-tone 2¼"-wide strips.

Color Option

Hoo's in the forest? Here's an interesting lesson in value and color placement. When Diane Harris looked at the line drawing of the quilt with no color at all, she saw trees all over the place! She gave the quilt a completely different look by emphasizing different parts of the design.

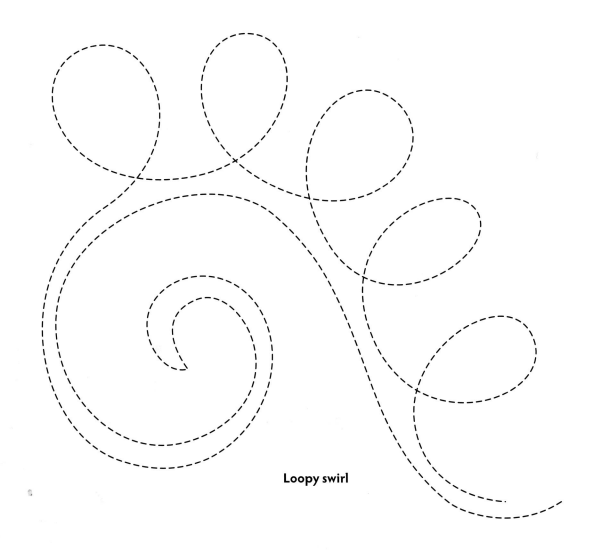

Loopy swirl

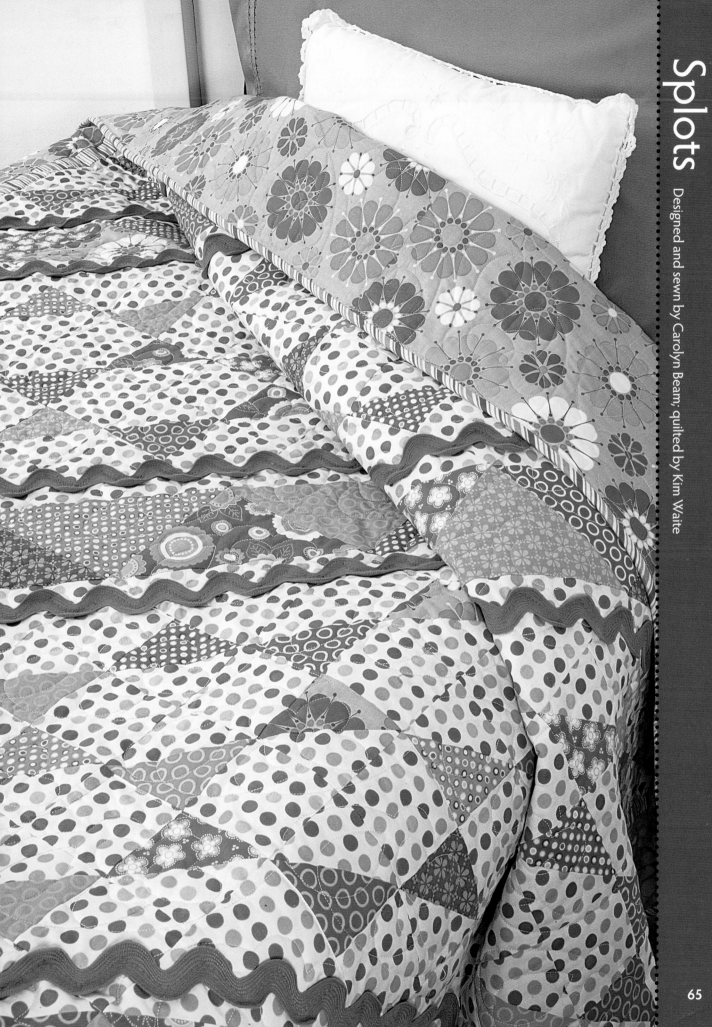

Stitch this quilt with a big splash of fun-filled color. Carolyn loved the fresh prints in these fabrics and wanted to showcase them in a simple design. The diagonal rows of giant rickrack add pizzazz! This quilt, made of simple half-square-triangle units in two different sizes, is ideal for using up scraps as well. Just choose a background fabric for the polka-dot areas, and the rest can be as scrappy as desired.

Materials

Yardage is based on 42"-wide fabric.

3¼ yards white dotted fabric for blocks

2⅝ yards of light-teal print for outer border

2 yards *total* of assorted prints and tone-on-tone fabrics for blocks

1¼ yards of multicolored striped fabric for inner border and bias binding

5⅞ yards of fabric for backing

74" x 98" piece of batting

11⅝ yards of giant rickrack* (optional)

If your local quilt shop doesn't carry giant rickrack, it can be found at elegantstitches.com. Giant rickrack measures 1½" from tip to tip.

Cutting

From the white dotted print, cut:

69 squares, 3⅞" x 3⅞"

138 squares, 3½" x 3½"

24 squares, 6⅞" x 6⅞"

From the assorted prints and tone-on-tone fabrics, cut:

69 squares, 3⅞" x 3⅞"

24 squares, 6⅞" x 6⅞"

From the multicolored striped fabric, cut:

8 strips, 1½" x 42"

2¼"-wide bias strips to total 326"

From the light-teal print, cut *on the lengthwise grain:*

2 strips, 5½" x 83"

2 strips, 5½" x 69"

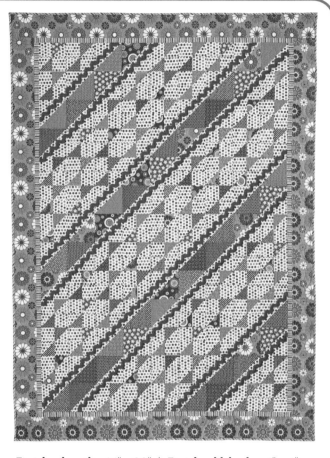

Finished quilt: 66" x 90" | **Finished blocks:** 6" x 6"

Making the Units and Blocks

1. Referring to "Half-Square-Triangle Units" on page 75, pair the white dotted and assorted 3⅞" squares to make 138 half-square-triangle units.

Make 138.

2. Sew two units from step 1 and two white dotted 3½" squares together as shown to make a block. Press the seam allowances as indicated by the arrows in the diagram. Make 69 blocks.

Make 69.

3. Pair the white dotted and assorted 6⅞" squares to make 48 half-square-triangle units as you did in step 1.

Make 48.

Assembling the Quilt Top

1. Arrange the blocks and half-square-triangle units into 13 rows of nine blocks each as shown in the assembly diagram. Sew the blocks into rows and press the seam allowances in opposite directions from row to row. Sew the rows together. Press.

2. Sew the multicolored-striped inner-border strips together and cut two lengths of 81" for the sides and two lengths of 59" for the top and bottom strips. Sew the side inner-border strips to the quilt and trim any extra length. Press the seam allowances

toward the border just added. Add the top and bottom inner-border strips in the same way. Repeat to add the light-teal outer border, sewing the 83"-long strips to the sides and the 69"-long strips to the top and bottom.

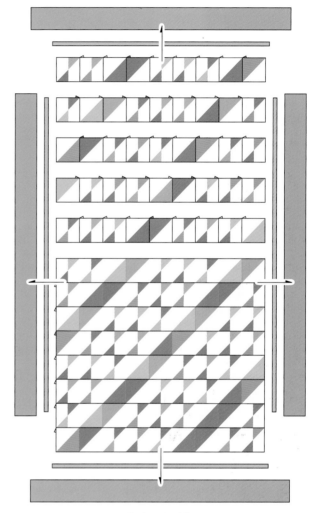

Quilt assembly

Quilting and Finishing

For more information on quilting and finishing your quilt, refer to "Basic Quiltmaking Lessons" on page 74.

1. Mark the continuous flower quilting design in the blocks and border, if desired, as shown in the quilting placement diagram on page 68.

2. Layer and baste together the backing, batting, and quilt top.

3. Quilt the marked motifs.

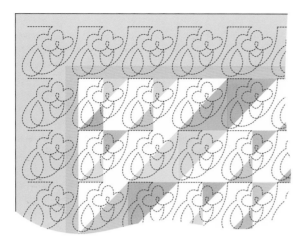

Quilting placement

4. If adding rickrack, use matching thread and a wide machine zigzag stitch to sew the rickrack approximately ¼" from each side of the large triangles. Tuck the ends under and stitch to secure.

5. Use the multicolored-striped bias strips to bind the quilt.

Color Option

Hedgehogs and woodland friends in a contemporary colorway can be found scattered across this crib-sized version.

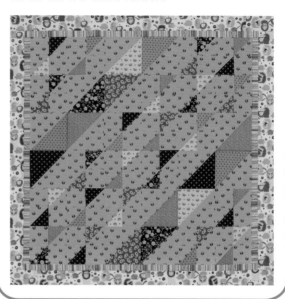

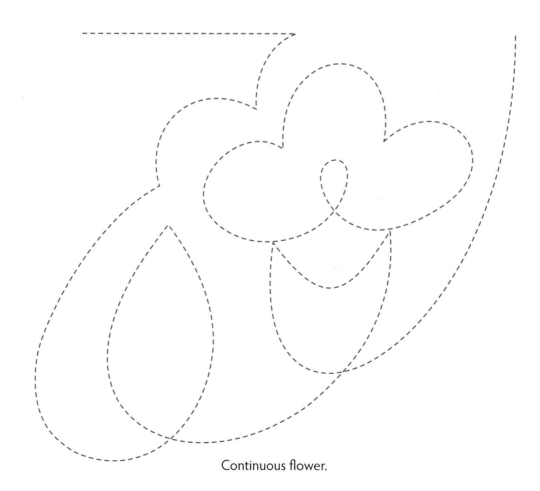

Continuous flower.

Improvise your way to a unique design! Diane began by piling fabrics that seemed to work together on her sewing-room floor. Over the months the pile grew as she added fabrics that she thought would fit in. One African fabric determined the direction of this quilt—its shapes reminded her of prairie points. The blocks are made with a time-honored method called string piecing, so named because you can use even the narrowest "strings," or strips, of fabric.

Materials

Yardage is based on 42"-wide fabric.

5⅝ yards *total* of assorted prints for blocks, prairie points, and binding

3⅛ yards of dark-blue solid fabric for blocks and border

4⅝ yards of fabric for backing

76" x 76" piece of batting

36 pieces, 10" x 10" of blank newsprint for foundations*

Approximately 100 buttons, ¼" to ½" diameter (1 for each prairie point)

5 black beads for birds' eyes (1 for each bird)

⅓ yard of 18"-wide fusible web (optional)

Or use your favorite foundation material.

Cutting

From the dark-blue solid fabric, cut *on the lengthwise grain*:

2 strips, 9" x 54"

2 strips, 9" x 71"

From the remainder of the dark-blue solid fabric, cut:

36 strips, 2" x 14"

From the assorted prints, cut:

150 to 220 strips and pieces, 1" to 6" x 2" to 8"

5 bird shapes (pattern on page 73)

96 to 100 squares, 2" x 2" or 3" x 3", for prairie points

2¼"-wide strips to total 286" for binding

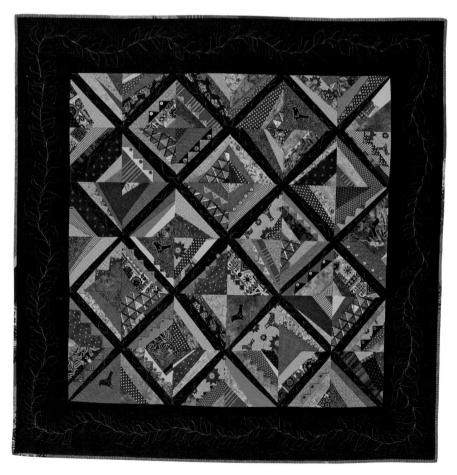

Finished throw: 68" x 68" | **Finished blocks:** 8½" x 8½"

About This Quilt

The blocks are pieced on a foundation of blank newsprint. If your machine's feed dogs have trouble feeding the newsprint, you can use a commercial foundation material or a muslin foundation. If you choose muslin, you'll need 2¾ yards to cut the 36 squares, 10" x 10".

Each block begins with a dark-blue solid strip across the diagonal center, but because this is improvisational piecing, your blocks will vary from the blocks in the quilt shown. The assorted prints should be cut into strips from 1" to 6" wide; any length is fine, as strips can be trimmed after they've been added.

Making the Blocks

1. Lay a dark-blue solid strip diagonally across a paper foundation, right side up as shown. Aligning raw edges, lay the next strip right side down on the dark-blue strip. Join the strips by sewing through all the layers ¼" from the raw edges. Flip the top strip open, trim any extra length, and press.

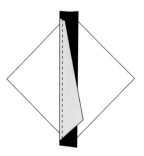

2. Continue to add strips from the center outward in both directions until the entire foundation has been covered. Trim the edges of the strips to create angles for interest, and add prairie points in the seams as desired, referring to "Prairie Points" on page 72. For the background behind the appliquéd birds, one side of the block can be made up of just one fabric.

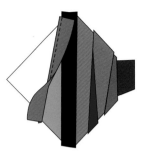

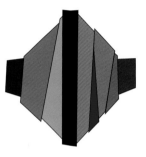

3. Trim the block to 9" x 9". Repeat steps 1–3 to make 36 blocks.

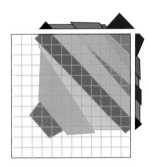

Trim to 9" x 9".

Make 36.

4. Prepare five bird shapes or as many as desired for fusible appliqué, following the manufacturer's instructions. Appliqué the birds to the blocks. Use matching thread and a tiny zigzag stitch to machine sew around the birds. Sew a bead to each bird for an eye.

Machine zigzag stitch

Assembling the Quilt

1. Referring to the assembly diagram, arrange the blocks on a design wall in six rows of six blocks each. Alternate the orientation of the blocks to create the design. Sew the blocks into rows. Press the seam allowances in opposite directions from row to row. Sew the rows together and press.

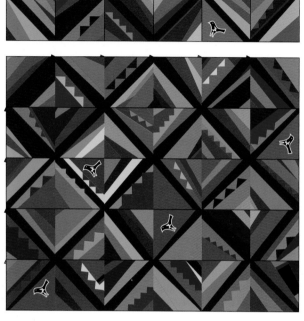

Quilt assembly

2. Sew the 9" x 54" border strips to the sides of the quilt and trim any extra length. Press the seam allowances toward the border. Add the 9" x 71" top and bottom border strips in the same way.

3. Carefully remove the foundation papers from the blocks.

Quilting and Finishing

For more information on quilting and finishing your quilt, refer to "Basic Quiltmaking Lessons" on page 74.

1. Layer and baste together the backing, batting, and quilt top.

2. Refer to the quilting placement diagram. Quilt various circles where the blocks meet as shown. Quilt freeform leaves in the dark-blue solid strips and in the border.

3. Bind the quilt using the assorted 2¼"-wide strips and sew a button to each prairie point.

Quilting placement

Prairie Points

For a set of prairie points, cut several matching 2" or 3" squares. Referring to the diagram, fold each square diagonally and press. Fold diagonally again and press.

Add the prairie points randomly to the blocks by matching their raw edges to the raw edges of a sewn and pressed strip before adding the next strip. The prairie points can be overlapped as much or as little as you like.

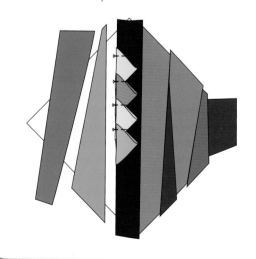

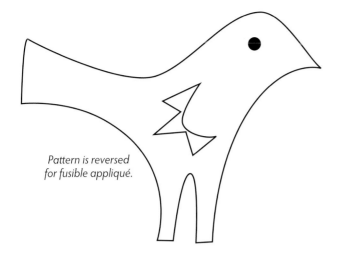

*Pattern is reversed
for fusible appliqué.*

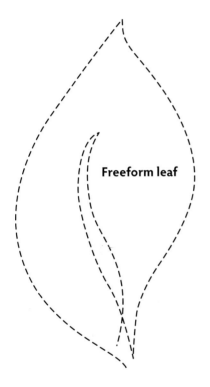

Freeform leaf

Color Option

The retro feel of these kitchen-themed fabrics plays against sultry batiks for an interesting table runner. Diane Harris used a fabric foundation in place of the newsprint, and quilted the runner without batting so it would lie flat on the table.

Basic Quiltmaking Lessons

We recommend that you read all of the instructions before starting a project, and that you cut and sew one block before cutting all of your fabric.

Use a rotary cutter, a mat, and an acrylic ruler to cut the shape to the size indicated in the cutting list. Each pattern lists the finished block size, which is ½" smaller than the unfinished block size because it does not include seam allowances.

Quilting Supplies

There are some basic supplies that you'll need for quilting. If you sew, you'll probably already have most of them on hand.

- Rotary cutter and mat
- Acrylic ruler: Many shapes and sizes are available; a good one to start with is 6" x 24" with ¼" and ⅛" markings.
- Scissors: separate pairs for paper and fabric
- Sewing machine
- ¼" presser foot
- Walking foot for machine quilting
- Darning foot for free-motion machine quilting
- Pins
- Ironing board and iron
- Marking tools (pencils, markers, etc.)
- Needles
- Thimble
- Safety pins
- Template plastic
- Thread

Preparing and Cutting Fabric

We recommend that you prewash your fabrics. A shrinkage factor is included in our yardage calculations.

Measure, mark, and cut binding and border strips before cutting other pieces from the same fabric. Cut larger pieces before cutting smaller ones. For best use of the fabric, cut your pieces so that the cutting lines are as close as possible.

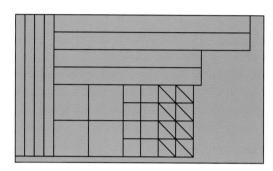

The straight edges of the strips, squares, and rectangles should follow the lengthwise (parallel to the selvages) or crosswise (perpendicular to the selvages) grain of the fabric. To find the grain line of your fabric for rotary cutting, hold the fabric with selvages parallel in front of you. Keeping the selvages together, slide the edge closest to you to one side or the other until the fabric hangs straight, without wrinkles or folds. Then lay the fabric down on your cutting mat and cut perpendicular to the fold line. Use this cut edge as your straight-of-grain line.

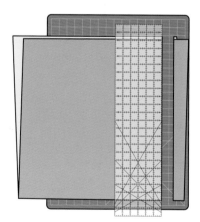

Many pieces can be cut from strips of fabric with rotary cutting. First, cut a strip of fabric the width needed. Then, crosscut the strip into pieces the required size.

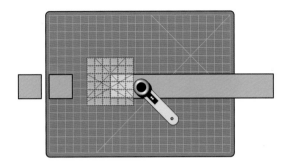

To cut using a template, place the template face-down on the wrong side of the fabric and trace with a sharp pencil. Reverse templates should be placed faceup on the wrong side of the fabric before tracing.

Machine Piecing

If you have a ¼" presser foot, align the cut edges of fabric with the edge of the presser foot. If not, place masking tape on the throat plate of your machine ¼" from the needle to use as a guide.

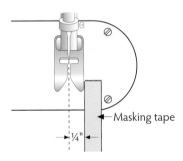

Masking tape

¼"

Half-Square-Triangle Units

This method of making half-square-triangle units eliminates the cutting and sewing of individual triangles. Each pair of squares will make two identical units.

1. With right sides together and the lighter fabric on top, pair a light and a dark square. Draw a diagonal line from corner to corner on the lighter square.

2. Stitch ¼" away from both sides of the line.

3. Cut along the marked line.

4. With the darker fabric on top, flip open the top patch and press the seam allowances toward the darker fabric.

Pressing

Press all seam allowances to one side, usually toward the darker fabric, unless otherwise instructed. When joining blocks and/or rows, press the seam allowances so that the seams will nest, which reduces bulk in the quilt top.

Squared Borders

Squared borders are added first to the sides of the quilt center, and then to the top and bottom. Lay the quilt top flat on a large table or the floor. Lay both side border strips down the vertical center of the quilt top and smooth carefully into place. Slip a small cutting mat under the quilt top (you'll need to do this at the top and the bottom edges) and use a rotary cutter and ruler to trim the border strips to the same length as the quilt top. Matching centers and ends, sew the border strips to the sides of the quilt top. Gently press the seam allowances away from the quilt center. Repeat this process along the horizontal center of the quilt top, including the just-added borders. Repeat for any remaining borders.

Mitered Borders

Mitered borders are added by sewing border strips to all sides of the quilt center, and then sewing each of the corners with a diagonal seam. When joining each border strip to the quilt, begin and end stitching ¼" from the corners of the quilt top, and backstitch.

Fold the quilt right sides together diagonally at one corner. Flip the seam allowances toward the quilt top, match seam lines, and pin through both layers about 3" from the corner. Place a ruler along the folded edge of the quilt top, intersecting the final stitch in the border seam line and extending across the border strip. Draw a line from the seam line to the outer edge of the border as shown.

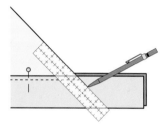

Pin the layers together along the marked line. Starting at the inside edge with a backstitch, sew along the line to the outer edge of the border. Trim the seam allowances to ¼" and press them open. Repeat for all corners.

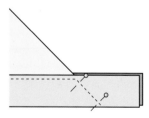

Marking Quilting Designs

Trace the quilting motif onto tracing paper. Place the tracing paper under the quilt top with a light source behind. Lightly mark the design on the quilt top with a hard lead pencil or a marker of your choice. Test any marking product for removability before using it on your quilt.

Straight lines may be marked as you quilt by using masking tape; remove it as soon as you have quilted along the edge.

Backing and Basting

Make the quilt backing 4" to 8" larger than the quilt top. Remove the selvages to avoid puckers. Usually two or three lengths must be sewn together. Press the seam allowances open. Place the backing wrong side up on a flat surface, stretch slightly, and tape or pin it in place. Smooth the batting over the backing. Center the quilt top right side up on top of the batting. Pin the layers as necessary to secure them while basting.

Basting for Machine Quilting

Machine-quilted tops can be basted with rustproof safety pins. Begin at the center and place pins 3" to 4" apart, avoiding lines to be quilted.

Basting for Hand Quilting

Beginning in the center of the quilt, baste horizontal and vertical lines 4" to 6" apart. Baste a diagonal line from the center to each corner.

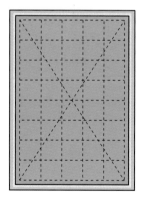

Quilting

Quilting in the ditch refers to quilting right next to the seam line on the side without seam allowances. Outline quilting refers to quilting ¼" from the seam line.

Machine Quilting

Before machine quilting, bring the bobbin thread to the top of the quilt so it doesn't get caught as you quilt. To do this, lower the presser foot, hold the top thread, and take one stitch down and up; lift the presser foot to release the thread tension and tug on the top thread to draw a loop of the bobbin thread to the top of the quilt. Pull the bobbin thread to the top. Lower the needle into the same hole created by the initial stitch, lower your presser foot, and start quilting. Use a walking foot for straight-line or ditch quilting. To free-motion quilt, drop (or cover) your feed dogs and use a darning foot. Start and end your quilting lines with ¼" of very short stitches to secure.

Hand Quilting

Hand quilting is done in a short running stitch with a single strand of thread that goes through all three layers.

Use a short needle (8 or 9 Between) with about 18" of thread. Make a small knot in the thread and take a long first stitch (about 1") through the top and batting only, coming up where the quilting will begin. Tug on the thread to pull the knotted end between the layers. Take short, even stitches that are the same size on the top and back of the quilt. Push the needle with a thimble on your middle finger; guide the fabric in front of the needle with the thumb of one hand above the quilt and with the middle finger of your other hand under the quilt.

To end a line of quilting, make a small knot in the thread close to the quilt top, push the needle through the top and batting only, and bring it to the surface about 1" away. Tug the thread until the knot pulls through the quilt top, burying the knot in the batting. Carefully clip the thread close to the surface of the quilt.

Binding

Baste around the quilt about ³⁄₁₆" from the outer edges. Trim the batting and backing ¼" beyond the edge of the quilt top.

Straight-of-Grain Binding

1. To prepare the binding strips, place the ends of two binding strips perpendicular to each other, right sides together. Stitch diagonally as shown and trim the seam allowances to ¼". Join all the strips in this way, and press the seam allowances open.

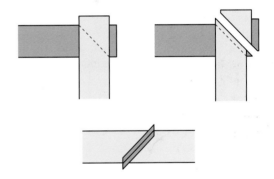

2. Cut the beginning of the binding strip at a 45° angle. Fold the binding strip in half lengthwise, wrong sides together, and press.

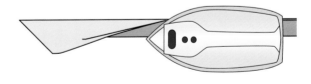

3. Starting in the middle of a side and leaving a 6" tail of binding loose, align the raw edges of the binding with the edge of the quilt top. Begin sewing the binding to the quilt using a ¼" seam allowance. Stop ¼" from the first corner and backstitch. Remove the needle from the quilt and cut the threads.

4. Fold the binding up, and then back down even with the next edge of the quilt. Begin stitching ¼" from the binding fold, backstitch to secure, and continue sewing. Repeat at all corners.

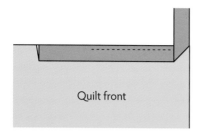

Quilt front

5. When nearing the starting point, stop sewing, remove the needle from the quilt, and cut the threads. Leave at least 12" of the quilt edge unbound and a 10" to 12" binding tail. Smooth the beginning tail over the ending tail. Following the cut edge of the beginning tail, draw a line on the ending tail at a 45° angle. Add a seam allowance by drawing a cutting line ½" from the first line; make sure it guides you to cut the binding tail ½" *longer* than the first line. Cut on this second line.

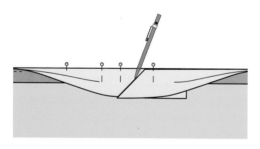

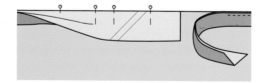

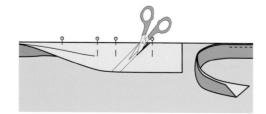

6. To join the ends, place them right sides together and sew, offsetting them ¼" as shown. Press the seam allowances open. Press this section of binding in half again, and then finish sewing it to the quilt. Trim away excess backing and batting *in the corners only* to eliminate bulk.

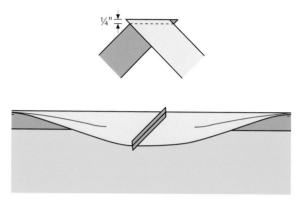

¼"

7. Fold the binding to the back of the quilt, enclosing the extra batting and backing. Blindstitch the fold of the binding to the back of the quilt, covering the line of machine stitching.

Quilt back

Bias Binding

Bias strips are cut at a 45° angle to the straight grain of the fabric. They're stretchy and therefore ideal for binding rounded corners or curves. They're also used when you want a plaid or stripe to be on the diagonal for binding.

1. Make your first cut by aligning a 45° guideline on your acrylic ruler with the cut edge or selvage of your fabric. Use this new bias edge to cut strips the required width.

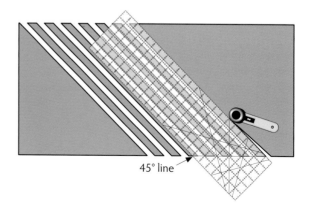

45° line

2. Join the bias strips as shown in step 6 of "Binding" on page 78. Then follow steps 2–7 of "Binding."

Hanging Sleeve

Sleeve edges can be caught in the seam when you sew the binding to the quilt. Cut and join enough 9"-wide strips of fabric to equal the width of the quilt. Hem the short ends of the sleeve by folding under ½", pressing, and then folding and pressing once more; topstitch close to the edge of the hem. Fold the sleeve in half lengthwise, wrong sides together, matching raw edges. Center the sleeve on the back and top of the quilt and baste. Sew the binding to the quilt. Once the binding has been sewn, smooth the sleeve against the backing and blindstitch along the bottom and ends of the sleeve, catching some of the batting in the stitches.

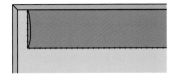